PET OWNER'S GUIDE TO THE
COCKATIEL

John Harley

RINGPRESS

Photography: Amanda Bulbeck.

Published by Ringpress Books Limited,
PO Box 8, Lydney, Gloucestershire,
GL15 4YN, United Kingdom.

First published 2000
©2000 Ringpress Books Limited. All rights reserved

ISBN 1 86054 116 X

Printed and bound in Hong Kong by Printworks International Ltd.

CONTENTS

1

Introducing
The Cockatiel

Delightful, beautiful, cheeky, companionable, hardy and gentle – these are but a few of the words that describe the cockatiel. Whether you want a parrot as a pet, an aviary inhabitant, an exhibition prospect, for breeding purposes, or for a combination of these, the cockatiel alone rivals the ubiquitous budgerigar. Small wonder that, after the budgie, it is the most popular parrot-like species in the world.

In some ways, the 'cocky' rates as the best bird for a beginner if they are first time parrot owners. Its larger size can be a definite plus. Furthermore, it has not yet deteriorated in many of the ways the budgie has over the years, as a direct consequence of its popularity as an exhibition bird. Many of the greatest names in aviculture, both of the present and of the past, have expressed the same opinions as I do about the virtues of this Antipodean avian gem.

HISTORICAL BACKGROUND

No-one is sure when the cockatiel was first taken from its Australian homelands to Europe. However, the famed English naturalist and artist John Gould is the man credited with penning the first accurate description of the species – then known as the corella. It is probable that the cockatiel was relatively well-established in Europe, within the aviaries of the more wealthy, by the late 1800s. The first breeding is said to have taken place in France during 1850. This was a decade after the first specimens were reliably documented as having arrived in Europe, along with the budgerigar.

By the early 1900s cockatiels were certainly being bred by an increasing number of people, though they were still quite expensive. As an indication of prices, a good pair of cockatiels was worth about three to four

The cockatiel, a native of Australia, is now a firm favourite in the west.

pounds during the early years of the 1900s. Imported and inferior stock could be obtained at a fifth of this price. Even so, that was still a lot of cash to the average fancier.

For all the vast numbers produced during the early years of the 20th century, the emergence of the cockatiel as a highly popular pet did not really happen until the 1960s. This was because more famous parrots, such as African greys, Amazons, and even the highly colourful parakeets of Australia and Asia, could be purchased at what were ridiculously low prices. The export ban on its fauna by the Australian

government during 1959 started a new era in bird-keeping circles.

CHANGING TIMES

Within a few years of the Australian ban, other countries followed suit. Formerly inexpensive exotic parrots soared in price. Most pet owners could no longer afford these, so the door was open for a lower cost species to fill the gap. By the late 1960s, the small parakeets of South America, the lovebirds of Africa, and the friendly cockatiel were gaining as popular pets.

Steadily, the cockatiel emerged as the sole challenger to the budgie. This was as it should be, given that the qualities of this parakeet had been so well known to aviary owners for so many years. The arrival of numerous colour and pattern mutations gave further impetus to the onward success of the cocky. Today it is enjoying unparalleled success in every area of the avicultural hobby.

SCIENTIFIC STATUS

The cockatiel, like so many other birds, has been moved from one group to another in formal scientific classifications tables during the years since it was first discovered. The average owner has little interest in such scientific wranglings. But the potentially serious hobbyist should be aware of where the cockatiel stands, zoologically, in relation to other birds and parrot-like species. This becomes important when reading scientific works, as well as when looking through multi-volume books to find the one that covers the parrot-like birds.

All birds are grouped together in a class of animals called Aves. This contains the 9,000 or so bird species known to exist at this time. The class is divided into many orders (27 of them) each housing birds displaying similar characteristics. There are orders housing gulls, pigeons, cuckoos, ostriches, ducks, owls, raptors (birds of prey) and so on. One of these orders is called Psittaciformes: it houses all the parrot-like species.

This order is divided into three families, each again containing those birds which display similar features, and are thought to have a common evolutionary path. The families are:

Loriidae – 55 species: Lories and lorikeets.

Psittacidae – 259 species: The true parrots – Parrots, Parakeets, and Macaws.

Cacatuidae – 18 species: Cockatoos.

Families are divided into *genus* (Pl. *genera*). In the family Cacatuidae there are five genus, and four of these contain the flamboyant cockatoos you may know of – the sulphur-crested, the black cockatoos, and so on. The fifth genus is called *Nymphicus* and contains just one species – this being our friend the cockatiel.

Its full scientific name is *Nymphicus hollandicus*. This name is unique to it within the entire animal kingdom. A species name is created by stating the genus the animal is in, then applying a name

Easy to keep, and full of character, the cockatiel is among the most popular of the parrots kept as pets.

to the species. This way, when the two names are used together, each species is uniquely identified.

AN UNUSUAL COCKATOO

The cockatiel is unusual in that experts are divided in deciding whether this bird is actually a cockatoo, albeit one rather different to most others, or a parakeet (parrot), albeit rather different to that group of birds. It displays features seen in both types but, on balance, is thought to be more cockatoo than parakeet. Such examples are known as being aberrant members of their group.

Cockatiels sport the crests typical of cockatoos, feed their offspring in the manner of cockatoos, share incubation duties as do cockatoos, and in other behavioural ways are clearly comparable with cockatoos. On the other hand, in their general body structure, tail-feather length, and powerful flying capabilities, they clearly resemble the parakeets.

Some experts have placed them among the broad-tailed parrots – the rosella group; others put them with the long-tailed parrots, such as the king and princess parrots. But, based on colour, crest, and behaviour, the cockatiel is probably in the most logical group based on all current knowledge.

PARROT OR PARAKEET

At this juncture, if you are new to the avicultural hobby, you may be wondering what the difference is between a parrot and a parakeet. Scientifically, there is no difference; the terms are interchangeable in many species, as they have been in this text. Generally, a short-tailed bird will be called a parrot, while one with a long tail is a parakeet. But, this said, the long-tailed 'parakeets' of

The typical crest of the cockatiel is a trait it shares with cockatoos.

Cockatiels are highly intelligent.

for most of us. Scientifically, a parrot is any member of the family Psittacidae. These are called the true parrots.

Members of the other two families are therefore not true parrots. They are parrot-like birds. But, given that the classification of parrots has changed time and again over the years, many species have been 'true' parrots at one time, and parrot-like at another! The cockatiel is therefore currently a parrot-like species, but it is still a parrot in the broad sense of its overall 'type' which is why it is in the order Psittaciformes (forms of parrots).

IS THE COCKATIEL FOR YOU?

In the following chapters you will find instruction and advice on all aspects of maintaining these marvellous birds. But, before you rush out and purchase one or more, you must carefully consider if they really are suited to your needs. Cockatiels are highly intelligent. They become very attached to their owners if kept as pets, and can live for over 20 years. They can learn to mimic words, tunes and other sounds. These very virtues have made them immensely popular.

However, many end up leading

Australia are normally called parrots, while the comparable birds of Africa, Asia and South America are called parakeets. Confused? Do not worry, it is not an important point.

You will also see the terms parrot and parrot-like used in the bird hobby, and may wonder what the difference is between these two types. This is an academic point for the purists, though not

The amount of time you spend caring for your cockatiel will be reflected in the bird's happiness and well being.

very unsatisfactory lives. They are housed in cages which are far too small, and are given liberty from their cages on a steadily reducing basis as the owner loses interest in them. This may be because the owner obtained the bird hoping it would be a great talker – a very bad reason to purchase any parrot.

It may also be because the cockatiel proves to be less friendly than this book suggests it should be. In this case, either the bird was poorly bred or, more likely, the owner simply did not devote the necessary time to it. There really is not a more placid and gentle parrot than the cockatiel. But it will only ever be what its owner makes of it.

Be sure you are prepared to invest your time, over a number of years, in your cockatiel. If you do, you will be as enthralled with it as are millions of other happy owners and breeders around the world.

2 Choosing A Cockatiel

'Buy in haste and repent at leisure' is a saying never more true than when applied to purchasing animals. There are a lot of gorgeous cockatiels to be had, but there are also a great deal that are worthless either as pets or breeding stock. Price alone does not guarantee you will obtain the ideal bird for your needs. You must go about the purchase process in an objective, dispassionate and patient manner. Objective, because you want the bird to meet your expectations. Dispassionate, because you must not purchase out of pity. Patient, so you do not buy on impulse, or out of frustration at not quickly finding exactly the right cockatiel.

OBJECTIVE NEEDS

Although the needs of a pet cockatiel are very comparable with those of an aviary, breeding or exhibition bird, there are a number of differences. Your first decision is to define the sort of bird you want. Do not think that a cockatiel bought as a pet may automatically be good enough to breed from or exhibit. You are likely to be very disillusioned. Likewise, an excellent breeding bird may not make an equally fine exhibition bird. Most certainly, not all show birds make good breeding stock.

Having defined the purpose of the bird, you must next consider the numerous factors that are important in choosing your particular bird, plus those which apply to all cockatiels. As each of the following topics is discussed you should make notes on the attributes you want in your cockatiel. Arrange them in an order of priority.

COCK OR HEN

From a pet perspective, the cock is generally regarded as the best choice. He usually becomes more accomplished at mimicking speech, whistling and other sounds. His crest is usually somewhat taller, his colours more striking. However, it is not always easy to sex these birds before their first moult at about six months of age. As a pet is best obtained as a youngster, you should not be unduly disappointed if your cock turns out to be a hen (see Sexing in the chapter on colours).

AGE TO PURCHASE

As a general guideline, and especially for pet or breeding stock, it is best to obtain a youngster within weeks of it having become fully independent of its parents. This means it will be seven or more weeks old. Once in adult feather, at about six months, it is almost impossible to determine a cockatiel's age.

A young bird is easier to train, has no unwanted bad habits, is easier to adjust to your favoured diet, and will have its entire life-span to spend with you. From a breeding viewpoint, you are able to monitor and influence its development, and it will be very settled when it is old enough to be bred from.

There is rather more to be said in favour of obtaining an exhibition prospect after it has moulted. You are able to see how its breeding and early potential is being converted into reality.

QUALITY

If the cockatiel is to be a home pet, it is not important that it is of the highest standard from an exhibition viewpoint. If its markings are less than perfect, or if its crest is not up to show standard, this will not affect its potential to be a great pet. What it must be is a sound, healthy, typical cockatiel with a friendly, chirpy outgoing personality.

A breeding bird must have better quality (conformation + breeding potential), while a show bird must have outstanding visual appearance.

COLOUR

The plumage of the wild type of cockatiel (called the normal) is very attractive, being a combination of grey, white and yellow, with a splash of orange on the cheeks. The cock's colours are more vivid than those of the hen. Apart from the wild colour pattern, a number of most beautiful mutations have appeared over the years and been developed to a high standard. We will discuss

Pet, show or breeding stock? Decide what you want from your cockatiel before making your choice.

these in the next chapter. Colour should never override health as a priority in any bird.

This means you must never pick a particular bird because it has the colour pattern you want, when either its health, conformation or temperament are questionable. Be patient, the perfect bird in the colour you want is out there; you just need to see more birds before you find it.

If you are thinking of breeding, colour will be an important consideration in your initial breeding stock, particularly if finances are a factor now and later on. The various mutations will be more costly to purchase, some very much more so than the wild type. However, in turn they will command more when it comes to selling surplus stock. It costs no more to keep and feed desirable mutants than it does those of wild type.

It makes eminent sense to make colour a priority in a new breeding programme. But some normals are always worth keeping. In terms of 'type' they invariably excel. They can be useful for maintaining conformation in a breeding stud.

Before you begin visiting pet shops and breeding aviaries to obtain a cockatiel, you are strongly recommended to visit one or two cockatiel, foreign bird or parrot shows. At such exhibitions, depending on their size, you will probably see every colour and feather pattern currently available in these birds.

The quality of the birds will range from sound to outstanding,

Normal Grey: The cock can be distinguished by his bright yellow face markings.

so you will have a mental yardstick against which you can judge the birds you see when you start your search for the perfect pet. If you are looking for breeding and exhibition stock, this will be the best place to start. Birds shows are advertised locally, and they are also

Pied: Patches of colour on a solid-coloured bird.

announced in national avicultural magazines available from your newsagent.

The following descriptions of the colours and patterns are not detailed. But they will give you a basic idea of what they are. The many colour illustrations in the text convey more than words the full beauty of a number of these varieties.

WILD TYPE (NORMAL GREY)

The body is grey, the outer wing edges white. The underside of the male tail-feathers is grey-black, that of juveniles and adult females barred with yellow. Beak, feet and

Pearl: This pattern occurs over the back and the wings.

legs are grey, the eyes dark-brown. The cheeks and throat are yellow, as is the crest. The ear coverts are orange. There is an area of white on the crown that wraps around the ear coverts to the throat. The female is a much paler version of the male in her head colours; immatures being similar to the female.

Sexing of the mutant colours follows that of the normal grey, but will be more difficult in those birds which display no melanin. In certain instances, where sex-linked colours are involved, it is possible to determine the sexes while they are still in the nest. Explaining the reasons is beyond the scope of this book – you are referred to more detailed works that discuss the genetics of cockatiels.

LUTINO

This is a beautiful variety, being varying depths of yellow, but with some white feathers, or suffusion, in all but the most outstanding show birds. The cheek patches are still orange, the eyes are red, the peak horn coloured, the legs pinkish. The same variety, if it displays more white than yellow, is often called an albino.

This would not be incorrect,

Albino birds have red eyes

because the mutated gene creating these apparently different colours is the same. What it does is to remove all melanin (dark) pigment, but does not affect yellow or red pigment. Breeder selection over a number of generations can increase or decrease the amount of yellow, thus producing the yellow or the partial albino.

ALBINO

Like the lutino, this is a very striking cockatiel. It is pure white with red eyes. However, unlike the albino just discussed (which is a true partial albino in the genetic sense) this albino is artificial. This means it is the result of combining

Cinnamon. Varying shades of brown replace the grey areas of the Normal Grey.

more than one mutation (Ino [lutino/albino] and whiteface) to produce a bird that has the appearance of being a true albino.

PIED

This variety displays varying amounts of white, yellow and grey in its plumage, the mutant gene having the effect of removing some of the dark pigments. It is a pattern rather than a colour. As with pieds in all animals, it is an extremely variable mutation. Some examples can look almost normal grey, with just the odd speck of white, others almost white and yellow with just a few grey areas. But most will be somewhere between these extremes.

PEARL

This is not a colour mutation but one which, as in the pied, affects the deposition of colour in the feathers; thus it is a pattern. The effect is to remove dark pigment in parts of the feathers so they produce a scalloped appearance. The outer part of the feather is grey (or the appropriate colour if in a mutational bird, such as cinnamon) and there is a yellow or white centre.

It is a very variable pattern, being neat and clear in some, but very blotched in others. As with most mutations, it can be combined with others to create interesting composite birds – those that are a mixture of mutations.

*White faced
Pearl Pied.*

CINNAMON

In this variety the grey areas of the normal grey are replaced by varying shades of brown, some being grey-brown, others fawnish, yet others cinnamon, its official show bench name. The colour can be combined with the pied, pearled and other mutations.

SILVER

This mutation has the effect of

Cockatiels are sociable birds and enjoy each other's company.

diluting the grey of the normal grey to produce a slightly lighter-coloured bird. It is unusual in that it has two forms. One is the single factor where the dilution is not as effective as in the double dose (double factor). The very lightest of silvers can be extremely attractive, showing only faint markings on a white ground. The silver colour variety is also produced by another mutation.

But, for the average pet owner, the genetic base of the colour has little importance.

WHITEFACE

The arrival of the whiteface mutation some years ago was quite an event. This mutation has the effect of removing both yellow and orange, thus leaving the head in white, and the body in grey and white with no yellow. In combination with the lutino, it creates the all-white false albino. It is a more costly variety than the others discussed.

In more recent years, the yellowface mutation has appeared. In this, the orange cheek patches are replaced by yellow to create another interesting and striking variety that can be combined with other mutations.

OTHER MUTANT VARIETIES

The varieties discussed are the ones you will most likely see in the average pet shop or breeder aviaries, some being more readily available than others. But a new mutation can appear at any time, in any owner's breeding stock. Additionally, existing mutations can be combined in very many ways to produce new varieties. At present there are fallows, which are

like light-coloured cinnamons.

There is the pastel, which looks just like a yellowface, but breeds differently, and there is the so-called olive. One day a melanistic (black) cockatiel may be produced and this will open up all sorts of possibilities. Certainly, the future for colour breeding in these birds continues to offer tremendous scope.

ONE OR MORE

If you will be devoting a great deal of time to your cockatiel, it is not necessary to obtain a companion for it. However, if you can afford the cost of two birds, you will find they provide twice the fun. They will be able to keep each other company when you are not with them. Two cocks, hens, or one of each will work because these avians are gregarious by nature.

WHEN AND WHERE TO PURCHASE

You can purchase these birds at any time of the year because, under artificial conditions of light and heat (as in a birdroom), they breed year-round. However, the late spring to summer is when they are most plentiful. Prices may be a little more competitive during this period.

If you are only seeking a nice pet bird, your local pet or bird shop will usually be able to meet your requirements – for both the bird and all necessary supplies. If you require breeding or exhibition stock, the breeder is the obvious source. You will want birds of known quality, which carry a closed leg ring that indicates the year the bird was hatched.

ASSESSING THE SELLER

There are good and bad pet shops and breeders. It is important that you assess them and their stock with a critical eye. Those which have been recommended are a good place to start. They can usually be relied upon to give you a nice bird at a fair price. The following are sound indicators of a good or bad supplier:

- The premises should be clean with no undue smell. Open sacks of seed should not be evident (risk of rodent and other fouling).
- Cages should look smart and very clean. Perches should not be caked in dried faecal matter, nor show signs of excessive wear. Water and seed should be in clean, uncracked containers.
- There should be adequate ventilation in the area of the birds, and it should also be light and cheerful.
- Cages should not be overcrowded so that birds are pressed against each other on perches, because they have no option if they want to rest on a perch.
- The birds should be lively and look very fit, with none of them being hunched in a corner, or on a perch, all fluffed up, when the rest are on the move.

ASSESSING THE BIRD

The signs of ill health are discussed in the health care chapter. Here it can be said that a fit cockatiel will appear lively and display no problems in climbing branches or moving from perch to perch.

Here is a useful tip. Even unwell birds may be spurred into action if you approach the cage or aviary suddenly and closely. Stand back some feet and allow the birds to settle down. Now study them to see if any show signs of lethargy and general disinterest in what the others are doing.

Always look carefully at the plumage; it is a really good indicator of fitness and health. It should be sleek and tight against

Plumage is a good indicator of a bird's general health.

the bird (unless the bird is in a rest position on one foot). A flaky, dry appearance, with numerous missing or broken feathers, is not a bird you want.

THE COST

Do not go looking for the cheapest cockatiel in town, for that price is what will be reflected in its health and suitability as a pet. Check with numerous stores and breeders to establish the going rate. Be sure to compare like with like, meaning in respect of age, sex (if known), colour, and whether it is hand-reared (always more costly).

If you have assessed the seller correctly, and are honest in telling them exactly what you want, you will generally obtain the right bird at a fair and realistic price. If you go looking for bargains you are much more likely to be sold a lemon.

3 *Setting Up Home*

It is strongly recommended you obtain the housing for your cockatiel before you purchase any birds. This would be obvious if you were planning to have aviaries, but not so obvious with an indoor pet. The reason for this is that, if the cage is obtained on the same day as the cockatiel, your choice may be limited. You could, in your eagerness to return home with your new pet, be tempted to make a purchase you later regret – expedience should never be placed ahead of desired suitability.

Visit numerous stores to select the right home for the new family member. It can be furnished and placed in its best location after due thought has been given to this. You are then ready to concentrate your energies into purchasing the perfect cockatiel.

CAGE DESIGN

By far the best design for any birdcage is one that is of a rectangular shape where the length is greater than the height. Tall, round cages, or those with ornamental Victorian-style triple-domed tops look interesting, but represent totally wasted space from the bird's standpoint. All birds fly horizontally, albeit at angles. None fly vertically, so, when in a limited space, length should be the major consideration.

True, a cockatiel can hardly fly in the typical cage, but it should be able to flutter from one perch to another. If a cage meets the minimum length requirement, but is very tall, this is fine as it gives the pet ample climbing as well as flutter space.

In reality, you will find that most commercially-made wire cages suited to cockatiels are in fact taller than they are long. They are produced on the assumption that residents will be given out-of-cage flying and exercise time.

CAGE DIMENSIONS

The first comment here is that if you are not prepared to allow your cockatiel out of its cage on a daily basis to exercise in your home, or in one of the rooms, you should not keep one of these birds as a pet. If they are not allowed out, then they are reduced to being ornaments.

Having accepted that your cockatiel must be allowed out daily, then the cage becomes only the sleeping and feeding quarters. However, it should still be as large as possible. The minimum size should be such that its depth must be wider than the bird's wingspan, so the wings, when being exercised, can be fully stretched without touching the bars.

When perched, there should be at least two clear inches above the bird's crest, and double this between the tip of the tail and the cage floor. Taking 38cm (15in) as the length of a cockatiel (including crest), 36cm (14in) as its wingspan, and with a 5cm (2in) rise between two perches, then the cage height must be a minimum of 58cm (23in) tall, 46cm (16in) deep and about 76cm (30in) long.

As the cage should be fitted with a sliding tray (for uneaten foods and faecal matter) beneath the false wire floor, it will actually be slightly taller than the height given. Such a cage makes a fine home for a cockatiel. There is no shortage these days of excellent and roomy parrot cages designed to cater for the needs of the long-tailed species.

The cage should be viewed as feeding and sleeping quarters only.

CAGE FEATURES

The standard features of modern parrot cages offer you a host of options from simple to extremely luxurious – with pricing reflecting the features and quality of materials used in construction. Purchase the best cage you can afford. It will last the cockatiel's lifetime. The more practical its standard features, the easier it will be to keep clean, as well as being a flexible home. Here are features to consider:

- Choose one that has a large access door. This makes chores easy to attend to. Some are designed so the entire front panel folds down to create a landing platform-cum-play area. They still feature a door in the panel, thus are versatile. You can also have a cage in which the top opens to form a platform.

- In some, the feeder pots must be filled from within the cage. In others, they are of the swivel type. These can be replenished without opening the cage door.

- The larger units may come complete with both legs and roller castors – very useful when cleaning the floor under the cage.

- Finishes can be chrome, or of tough epoxy resin. The latter are available in various colours.

- Deluxe models will feature an extending exterior apron around the cage base to catch fruit, seeds and feathers that fall out of the cage bars – they are channelled back into the base. You can also purchase these as add-ons later, as well as plastic skirts to fit most cage sizes.

- Feeder pots may be plastic or stainless steel. Steel is the best.

- The distance between cage bars should be no more than 19mm (3/4in).

- Two perches are best. If they have variable diameters along their length this is even better for exercising the toes.

- Be advised that inexpensive cages soon tarnish and may have dangerous sharp projections on them. Welded joints may be of poor quality and attract bacteria.

- Beware of purchasing used cages. Spores and bacteria can lay dormant for long periods.

If you are keeping your cockatiels in an aviary, you have to plan the whole environment so it is suitable for their needs.

As an alternative to a cage you could, if space permits, purchase an indoor flight. These provide ample opportunity to be attractively furnished, will accommodate a number of birds and, in the galvanised form, may cost less than the deluxe style cages discussed.

Today, purchasing a cage for your pet can be like buying a car or house; there are so many options and models to choose from. Always give space, ease of cleaning, and expected longevity a high priority.

AVIARIES AND LAWS

Many bird owners, for numerous reasons, may not wish to keep their birds in the home as pets. Rather, they prefer to see them in garden aviaries. In these, the birds live a much more natural life, and the aviary itself can become an integral part of the garden landscape. If you are one of these people, your first thoughts must be directed to whether or not you can legally have an aviary. The factors that will decide this will be:
1. Whether you live in rented or leased property, either privately or council owned.
2. The type of area you live in if the house is your own.
3. The size of the proposed aviary.
4. The type and number of birds

being kept (potential noise nuisance).

5. The closeness of the aviary to another home (hygiene considerations).

6. The purpose of the aviary – commercial breeding or hobby.

Generally, a modest aviary classed as portable will not be a problem. But any structure regarded as permanent will usually require building, and maybe other, permissions – which involve detailed plans being supplied to the appropriate authorities.

Some housing developments have no problem with small aviaries; others may not accept them at all. Have your deeds checked, or contact the council if you live in one of their properties. If you fail to look into this matter, and erect an aviary, you could be told to dismantle it and dispose of the birds. Always stay within local laws.

AVIARY COCKATIELS

The cockatiel vies with any bird as an ideal aviary resident. Unusually for a parrot of its size, the cocky is quite safe with even the smallest of finches. If anything, you must take care you do not include it in a mixed parrot collection with birds that may bully it – which means

most parrots, even the small but often pugnacious lovebirds.

Generally, it will cohabit with many of the smaller Australian and Asian parakeets. It can be mixed with numerous doves, quail, and softbilled birds of its own size or smaller. But it must always be remembered that any bird is an individual and may not behave in the generally accepted manner. This means that some normally placid species can have the occasional aggressive individual.

Any group of birds, be they of mixed or single species, must always be observed as individuals when each is added to an existing collection. Just one bully can cause total havoc in an aviary, the more so if any of the others are in a breeding state. Even the cockatiel can be temperamental if it has youngsters in a nest within a species or in a mixed aviary.

A COMPLETE ECOSYSTEM

Another point that must never be forgotten is that all birds are territorial to a greater or lesser degree. The size of an aviary will have considerable bearing on how many birds will cohabit peacefully in it. There is no formula for deciding this. A mixed aviary collection must be developed slowly; it will develop its own social society. Just one bird too many may be enough to upset the peaceful balance. The aviary is a total ecosystem in itself. It must be managed as such by your observations and experiences as they are gained.

AVIARY DESIGNS

An aviary may be designed for one or more purposes, so it is important not to rush into building one. Indeed, a great deal of planning should go into any worthwhile aviary. For example, a display aviary will normally have its flight across your line of vision – so you can enjoy watching the birds from a distance and this blends the aviary into the general landscape. Breeding aviaries will normally be end-on from your main viewing place, so you can observe many flights at the same time.

You can combine these two objectives by placing a display aviary between breeding aviaries so they are on either, or both, of its flanks. The potential designs and layouts of single or numerous aviary complexes is legion. You are advised to visit and gather catalogues from companies who build aviaries. Contact a number of local breeders to see their layouts. Most will be delighted to show you these, and offer useful tips. Always work your ideas out on paper – it is much easier to move things round, add to, or cancel them at that stage rather than having to alter the real thing!

THE AVIARY SITE

Many beginners erect aviaries on unsuitable sites; this is only realised when the aviary is up and running. Unless you are very lucky, and have no limits on your budget, there will invariably be compromises. If you appreciate the problems from the outset, you are less likely to make major errors. Here are the prime considerations, some or all of which will apply to any proposed aviary location.

1. The Terrain.

This will either be flat or sloping to some degree of steepness. Avoid low spots on sloping ground. They will be damp or even flooded after rains. Excavating for levelness on mid-slopes will be time-consuming. If much rubble has to be removed will this be easy to do access-wise? Effect trial digs to establish how much rock or rubble lies under the topsoil.

Birds are territorial, so you must try to get the right number of birds who will live together in peace.

2. Where To Avoid.
• Under overhanging branches of trees. After rains and snow the aviary will remain wet for days and become damp, thus encouraging fungus growth. Wild bird droppings from birds perched overhead will foul the flight. Falling autumn leaves will create more work. Rodents can gain easier access to the roof.
• Over utilities. Establish precisely where water, sewage and electrical pipes and lines run so, if these need attention, no part of the aviary will be on top of them!
• Difficult-to-view locations. It is always best if your aviaries are visible from the room you spend most time in. You can see what is

going on. As important, at night the aviaries are at less risk of being burglarised.

• Exposed sites. Do not locate the aviary where it will be subject to cold winter winds, rains and snows, nor to long hours of intense sunshine. Southerly aspects are favoured so early morning sunshine is on the aviary. Fortunately, if exposed sites are the only option, you can counteract these by using various windbreaks and canopies.

A final piece of advice with regard to the site is this. If you develop a growing interest in the hobby, does your initial site provide room for expansion? If you have two equally suitable sites, choose the one with expansion potential.

THE BASIC AVIARY

Having considered all aspects of the aviary location you can now apply thoughts to the aviary itself. All aviaries comprise three distinct parts. The base, the flight, and the shelter. Each should be considered as a unit unto itself. There are many options and factors to take into account depending on your needs, aesthetic inclinations, and budget.

At this time you should also consider supplying utilities to the aviary. They are not part of an aviary structure, but are best regarded as obligatory. Water and electricity will greatly ease day-to-day chores, while water sewage disposal is only marginally behind the other two as a useful facility.

THE BASE

This should extend beyond the perimeter of the aviary complex. The base of the flight should have a slight slope away from the shelter so that hose or rain water easily flows away. In order of preference, the base should be of concrete, slabs or gravel. Grassed or bare earth is a poor choice, giving rise to hygiene problems.

THE FLIGHT

Always make the flight as long as possible, especially for cockatiels, which are swift fliers. A minimum length should be 1.8m (6ft) which is also the minimum for height. 2.1m (7ft) is a better height from the aesthetic viewing standpoint. A flight where the roof slopes from 1.8-2.1m will attract the birds to the highest end for your better viewing

The weld mesh gauge (its thickness) should be 19G or less (thicker) and the hole size should

The more natural the environment, the better for your cockatiels.

ideally be 25x12.5mm (1x1/2in) to keep out all but small mice. Double meshing of adjoining flights, especially if these contain any aggressive species, is recommended to remove the possibility of cockatiel legs being bitten.

If the flight can be accessed direct from outside, a safety porch should be featured. You thus enter this, closing its door behind you, before you open the flight door. You will need a pop hole from the aviary to the shelter so birds come and go as they please. This should be hinged, or on a slider, so it can be closed if you wish to keep the birds in the shelter, or in the flight.

Place perches or a landing platform in front of the hole, which should be about 20cm (8in) square, or larger. At the shelter end of the flight it is beneficial to place tinted transparent stiff plastic over the roof. This provides shade and protection from wind and rain. Your birds can stay outside during showers, but not get a soaking, unless they want one for bathing. This sheeting can extend down the sides for extra protection during the colder months.

The wire mesh is best stapled onto a wooden framework to create panels. These can easily be dismantled for repair, replacement or extension needs. It enables the aviary to be taken with you should you move home. For longest life, and better viewing, paint the mesh with bitumen. The frame for the mesh should be 5x5cm (2x2in) and treated with a preservative.

The aviary bird may need additional warmth during the cold months.

The flight panels should be bolted directly into the concrete or slab floor, or onto a small decorative wall, which always looks nice. If you purchase a low cost pre-made aviary, be sure it is well secured to a base so it does not lift during gales.

THE SHELTER

The shelter, at its most basic, need be no more than a well-insulated wooden structure the birds can enter from the flights, and which contains perches and feeding platforms. Your access to this can be from within the flight or, via a safety porch, from outside the shelter. At the other extreme, and the most typical for breeders, it will be a birdroom. This will contain indoor flights the birds enter from the outside flights. It will also contain shelves, store cupboards and all the other things you are likely to need.

Shelters and birdrooms should be light and airy; birds do not like to enter darkened places, apart from which sunlight is an excellent disinfectant. Cockatiels do not need heated winter quarters in temperate climates. This said, you (and the birds) will no doubt appreciate some background heating during the coldest weather.

Good insulation and ventilation, easy cleaning considerations, and ample room are the keys to the ideal birdroom, both for you and the cockatiels.

FURNISHINGS

There are today so many appliances, feeders and extras you can purchase for your cockatiel that you may be overwhelmed by the choice. Here we will review a range of these, and the best types for these birds. As with most things, you will get what you pay for. It is always advisable to buy the best quality. They function better and have a longer life.

GOLDEN RULES

Whether in a cage or aviary there are golden rules you should apply. Never overcrowd the housing with furnishings. A priority must always be that the bird has ample free space in which to exercise its wings, and to move from perch to perch without having to avoid obstacles.

Do not waste your money on poor quality toys that are not only unneeded junk, but also potentially dangerous if they easily chip and are swallowed. Whenever a toy, feeder, or other appliance starts to crack, or becomes difficult to clean when its surface becomes tarnished or chewed, get rid of it. Not to do so greatly increases the risk of disease. This fact should never be underrated and, since most of the throw-away items involved are invariably low-cost, they are easy to replace.

Ensure toys and feeder vessels are never placed directly under perches where they will become fouled with faecal matter. For the same reason, never place perches under each other.

FOOD AND WATER CONTAINERS

The choice here is plastic, pot, or stainless steel either free-standing or clipped to the cage bars. Cockatiels are not destructive birds, so the better plastic containers work fine if clipped to cage bars. Those that can be replenished from outside the cage are preferred. Free-standing containers are best in pot or steel. They are less easily tipped over by these playful birds.

If you keep a number of cockatiels together, it is best to use a number of feeder pots at opposite ends of the cage or aviary feeding area. There are three advantages. It overcomes the

Feeding utensils can be clipped to the side of the cage or attached to a perch.

potential for a higher-ranked individual to always get first choice at the favoured items. It is also more economic. All birds tend to be wasteful feeders and will quickly throw out the less-favoured seeds. Having the staple foods in one dish, and the lesser ones in others, makes more sense, and less waste.

Finally, it makes the birds move

Provide a variety of different perches.

between feeders to obtain their rations. This is psychologically beneficial to them for they are working to obtain food, albeit at a low level of work!

PERCHES

Many bird owners do not give perches the attention they should. Commercial cages fit standard sizes, hopefully to suit a range of birds. The ones fitted may not suit a cockatiel. These birds require a diameter, as a guide, from 9.5-19mm (3/8-3/4in). Why the variation? If the bird continually lands on a perch of the same size, the same part of its foot will touch this. It may develop sores or

unwanted hardened skin. It needs variety to fully exercise its toes and nails. You can purchase variable-width perches, or simply sandpaper the fitted ones to feature variability. Fresh fruit or other non-poisonous branches will also provide natural perches.

Within aviary flights, the perches should be arranged at either end of the flight to provide maximum open flying space between them. Within the shelter, they should be arranged likewise. If made of doweling, they should lie in parallel and be arranged so each upper perch is set further back than the one below it.

Cockatiels enjoy playing with toys, but make sure you do not overcrowd the cage.

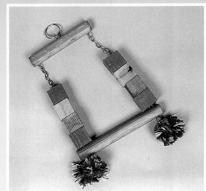

PLAYTHINGS

Strong lengths of rope with wood or plastic rings attached, sturdy ladders, bobbins, non-poisonous twigs, bells and climbing platforms are all ideal safe toys for these birds. Inexpensive plastic budgie toys soon clutter a cage. Birds can become infatuated with mirrors, so I do not recommend them. They may suppress the bird's willingness to develop strong relationships with other companion birds.

BATHS

Providing they are large enough for cockatiels, baths that clip on the cage door are very useful during hot weather and moulting periods. Birds love to bath – it keeps their feathers in great shape. Alternatively, purchase a mist spray. Once a week use tepid water to spray your pet in or out of its cage: they will love it.

In aviary flights, a large shallow earthenware dish with about 2.5cm (1in) of water will greatly amuse your pet. A birdbath with a gentle fountain is another option that will be both aesthetically pleasing and beneficial to the birds, as would a simple waterfall.

PECKING TRAY

In a large cage, or an aviary flight, a shallow tray 7.5cm (3in) deep, with holes in its base, can be thinly covered with coarse sand, crushed eggshell and various-sized gravel. This will be appreciated by a cockatiel. Sprinkle some seeds on it and the birds will enjoyed pecking over it much as they would on the ground in the wild. Hose it regularly to remove any faecal matter, and periodically replace contents totally.

BIRD NET

Aviary owners should have a bird net, especially if finches are kept with cockatiels. The net should have a large padded opening. It should not be of open-mesh type otherwise the bird's head, legs, toes and wings might be trapped and injured.

The advantage of a net is that it enables the bird to be caught quickly, rather than your having to chase around the aviary after it, which involves the risk that the bird might crash into the flight mesh or shelter wall. Pet or owner-friendly cockatiels can usually be caught without a net, but it is always worthwhile owning one.

IONIZER

In multi-pet homes, and in birdrooms, an ionizer is a most useful appliance. Available in a range of sizes and economical to run, they release negative ions that attract dust particles and bacteria. This makes the ions heavier than air and they fall to the nearest surface, so are easily wiped away. Ionizers also help to minimise odours. They are obtained from good pet stores and avicultural suppliers.

NIGHT-LIGHT

Whether in a house room or an aviary situation, a low wattage night-light (white or blue 8-25 watts) is recommended. This greatly minimises the risk of night-fright, a condition brought about by something startling the bird. It may then take flight in its panic and crash into the cage or aviary bars, or walls. The danger is that, apart from sustaining an injury, in aviary situations the bird may land on the floor of the flight on a cold night and not be able to see its way back to the shelter. Small, light-sensitive night-lights are excellent because they go on and off according to the amount of light landing on them.

Caring For Your Cockatiel

Feeding your cockatiels is not an exact science. Nor has the diet of any one breeder proved to be superior to that of all others. As a consequence, by having a basic understanding of nutritional requirements, you can rapidly develop your own regimen that will produce fit and impressive cockatiels. The basic diet of these birds is seed, which is the fundamental reason why many of the Australian species were so quickly established in breeding aviaries of the early hobby pioneers. However, even for the Australian species, a seed-only diet is far from being adequate to maintain excellent feather, breeding vigour, and general good health. So, the first thing to appreciate is that parrots should never subsist on a seed-only diet – as many unfortunate birds have done in the past, and continue, in some homes, to do to this day.

NUTRITIONAL OVERVIEW

The role of nutrition extends well beyond the narrow view that it is to maintain the metabolism of the individual. To eat, a bird must first find its food, then select which items it wishes to eat. These will be in a hierarchic order based on taste. For flock birds, such as cockatiels, feeding is also very much a social matter through which young birds learn to select those items beneficial to them. In the process, they learn to interact with their conspecifics.

Nutrition therefore embraces all aspects of a bird's life. This is often overlooked by pet owners, and those who try to convince us that complete diets in the form of powders, cubes, pellets and whatever will meet the total nutritional needs of our birds. Related to metabolic needs they may possibly do so, but what about the other aspects – the psychological need to make

The cockatiel eats by crushing the seed and then discarding the husk.

selections based on taste and texture? And can you be really sure that 'total' needs, even metabolically, are, in fact, being met? When you plan your cockatiel's diet, you should endeavour to balance this between items that are natural, and those which are commercial formulae based and developed on known needs to this point in time. By adopting such a policy you will be more likely to fulfil the total needs of nutrition.

BIRD DIGESTION

Having no teeth, a bird initially crushes any shell around its food. The shell, or husk, is discarded and the seed swallowed. Within the gizzard, which in seed-eating birds is well muscled, the food is crushed against pieces of grit which the bird swallows as it pecks over the ground. Once crushed to a paste-like consistency, the food continues on its journey down the digestive tract.

Two important points should be learned from this process. The seed husks are discarded. Many a poor pet has almost starved because the owner, seeing lots of husks in its seed dish, assumed these were whole, or assumed there were more seeds under the husks. Every day the husks should be blown from open seed pots. In the case of seed dispensers, the tube should be tapped daily to ensure its exit is not blocked, especially if it contains a mix that includes larger seeds such as sunflower.

It is vital your birds always have grit available to them. Some birds will not take this from pots, so scatter it over the cage floor or, if this is of mesh, place it on a tray as well as in a pot until you are sure the bird is taking it from this. That which is suitable for budgerigars or other small parakeets will be the correct size.

Cuttlefish bone is also essential to your cockatiel for its calcium content, while crushed oyster or eggshell can also be supplied to provide calcium and minerals. An iodine block, crushed charcoal, and a pinch of rock salt, are other beneficial mineral additives.

SEEDS
For one or two pet birds, packaged budgerigar seed, small parakeet mixes, or those prepared by the pet shop, are the best way

A mix of seeds suitable for a cockatiel.

Grit is an essential item.

to buy. Breeders should purchase individual seed types and make up their own mixes. As a guide, and all breeders have their preferred ratios, a mix should contain 40-50 per cent canary, 30-40 per cent millet, and 20-30 per cent other seeds.

Always obtain the best polished seeds that are as dust-free as possible. It is best to purchase no more than a month's supply at a time, to minimise the potential for the seed constituents to deteriorate. Never feed a seed that is split and has sticky sap oozing from it – this is poisonous. Store seed in a well-ventilated, cool, dry place.

The following are the most important seeds to feed your cockatiel.

Carbohydrate-rich seeds and grains: canary (Moroccan is best), millet (white and panicum is preferred), millet spray (French Anjou or Chinese), maize, oats, groats, wheat, and barley.

Protein and fat-rich seeds: peanut (not salted), pinenut

Soaked seed is appreciated.

Millet is a great favourite, but rations should be limited.

(Russian is preferred), linseed, maw, niger, sunflower (striped is preferred to white or black), safflower, and hemp.

There are, in fact, many other seeds that can be fed, but those listed are the ones most used in the hobby and available from pets shops and seed merchants. Always exercise care in feeding high-protein/fat seeds, especially to a house pet. Such cockatiels can soon become obese: if this is noticed, reduce this type of seed. Likewise, do not overfeed millet spray. The birds can glut excessively on this and spoil their appetite for other needed food. Sprays can be fed dry or soaked in water for 24 hours, rinsed, then fed – your birds will love them. One spray a week is sufficient.

SOAKED SEED

When a seed is immersed in water for 24-36 hours it begins to germinate. Its protein content increases and it is more easily digested. Once soaked, it must be rinsed thoroughly. It is a great pick-me-up and valuable for birds with youngsters in the nest. That which is not eaten within a few hours should be discarded because it soon attracts bacteria.

Cockatiels may have difficulty in coping with large grain, so this should be crushed or soaked so it will be more acceptable. You should also soak dried foods, such as fig, apricot, peas, lentils and their like before feeding them to your birds so they do not swell in the bird's digestive system and create problems.

FRUIT

Although cockatiels will not consume vast amounts of fruit, they do, nonetheless, enjoy them. Fruits are very important because they supply needed vitamins and make a welcome texture change from seed.

Popular examples are apple, orange, grape, honey melon, kiwi, banana, blackberry, strawberry, elderberry, peach, apricot, fig – in fact most things that you are likely to find on a fruit stall. Avoid avocado. Make a sliced salad of a few and you will soon find out which are and are not liked by your birds, all of which have both common and individual palates.

A word of caution. If your cockatiel is not already being fed fruits when you obtain it, start with very small amounts. Never provide a sudden glut, which is sure to create digestive problems. This advice applies to any new dietary item.

VEGETABLES AND GREEN FOODS

The comments made about fruits apply to this group of foods as well, indeed to all other non-seed foods. Examples of vegetables and green foods are boiled potatoes, carrots, celery, spinach, beet, beans, peas, lentils, broccoli, kale, red or green peppers, and asparagus, to name but a few. Be sure fresh foods are rinsed before feeding, to remove any residual crop sprays and unwanted parasitic or bacterial visitors.

WILD FOODS

Within this group come dandelion, chickweed, various seeding grasses, plantain, and, of course, twigs and small branches from fruit trees and those such as willow, and hawthorn. Twigs provide valuable cellulose fibre, and the birds love playing with them while they eat. Wild plants should only be gathered from your garden or other areas where there is minimal risk of fouling by car fumes or animals. Rinse before

A variety of fruit and vegetables will be appreciated.

Dandelion.

*Chickweed.
Rinse well before feeding.*

feeding. If in doubt about wild plants, leave them well alone until you establish if they are safe for birds.

OTHER FOODS

Oven-baked bread, small dog biscuits, boiled egg, cheese, yoghurt, plain cake, and even the occasional small hard bone (not rabbit or chicken) with some meat on it, will be variously enjoyed by your cockatiel according to palate. Breeding birds may be offered small quantities of bread soaked in milk, or you could try one of the formulated rearing foods available from avicultural specialists.

PELLETS

The feeding of commercial pellets, especially in the USA, has increased considerably in recent years. They have the advantage of convenience, and claim to be a complete food. However, birds need to be converted to these foods because, given free choice, most birds will always prefer their food in a natural form. Nonetheless, they can become a useful dietary item.

The main problem with convenience foods is that they deprive the bird of choice. For most parrot owners, part of the joy of owning them is surely in

Feed small amounts, and clean up leftovers regularly.

watching the way they take obvious pleasure in searching through the daily menu to see if it contains any of their favourite items, and the pleasure they derive from eating these.

HOW MUCH TO FEED

Seed and water must be available to your cockatiel at all times. During cold weather, in unheated shelters, be sure the water does not become frozen. If gravity-fed inverted water bottles are used, be sure the water in the spout is not frozen, even though that in the bottle appears fluid.

Fresh foods are best given in the early morning or late afternoon when they will not sour as quickly as during midday periods in the warmer months. Feed only those amounts that are eaten within a few hours. Always remove any which has been left uneaten. Breeding birds will require greater amounts of food, especially when chicks are in the nest.

HEALTH CARE

A cockatiel's health will be directly controlled by its environment, nutrition, mental state, opportunity to exercise, and by genetic make-up. You can do nothing to change its genetic make-up and the effects this may have on the bird. But all the other factors are directly under your influence.

By ensuring that husbandry standards are maintained to a high level, you greatly reduce the risk of your bird becoming seriously ill. Should it show any signs of a problem, the standards you maintain will mean you will quickly notice when something is wrong. This is what keeps the vet bills down and avoids illnesses.

There are, today, many vets with speciality knowledge of birds. Once you obtain your cockatiel, locate such a vet – do not wait until the vet is needed. Nor should you try to diagnose/treat problems. Let the vet attend to this using modern diagnostic

equipment. If you attempt to do these things you could be very wrong. The result could be a dead pet. In an aviary situation it could result in the loss of many birds.

KEEP IT CLEAN

Cleaning is an area of husbandry that is all too easy to neglect, especially in birdrooms that contain many cockatiels housed in worn cages, and buildings that are very labour-intensive, which means it is difficult to clean walls, floors, surfaces and there are no utilities.

It is also easy to overcrowd birdrooms, which increases the need to devote more time to cleaning. But owners are not always able to do this because they have too many birds to care for. It becomes a vicious circle, only corrected by scaling down the stud.

For a pet owner there are no mitigating circumstances. The cage should be tidied daily and thoroughly cleaned each week. This must include cage bars on which birds often wipe their beaks – a prime way bacteria are able to gain access to their respiratory and other systems – as well as the perches.

Cracked and chipped feeders or

Keep a close check on your cockatiel so that you will spot any problems at an early stage.

water containers should be replaced. Keep spares on hand. Aviary owners should never allow a compost heap anywhere near the aviary. It will become a source of bacteria, fungus and flies. Bags of debris removed from the cages should be disposed of the same

Cage cleaning must be undertaken on a regular basis.

very different in their properties. This especially applies to dangerous chemicals in them, a prime example being the ammonia in faecal matter. This is very harmful to the respiratory system. If not removed on a regular basis it can reach dangerous levels you are not aware of.

Likewise, a cage facing on to an open exterior door is subjected to rapid temperature fluctuations (draughts) that induce chills. Cages not shaded from direct sunlight are also subject to such fluctuations, as are those near heaters, air-conditioning outlets and cooling fans. In birdrooms, the lowest level of tiered cages may have a very different temperature from the higher ones. Multi-tiered banks of cages can become a health hazard.

day. Always wash your hands before and after attending cleaning chores, feeding, or handling your birds or other pets – and especially after gardening. Cleaning must be scrupulous.

CLIMATIC CONTROL
The cage in which a bird lives is its local climate. The room or aviary is its general climate. They can be

VENTILATION
A major cause of problems in birdrooms is inadequate ventilation. It results in a steady build-up of pathogens, more so when conditions are humid. Be sure there is a steady, non-draughty, flow of air through the building. Placing ventilation ducts low down at one end and high up at the other will help to create a good current. Extractor fans will assist this.

HOSPITAL CAGE

Breeders should have at least one hospital cage. Any easy-to-clean and roomy box cage will work fine. It should contain two perches, one at normal height, one close to the floor for the very sick bird. A shallow tray of water at one end will help maintain humidity during dry air periods. This is important when treating egg-bound hens.

A thermometer inside the cage, but protected from the bird's beak, is essential. You also require a dull emitter infra-red lamp – never the heat lamps than produce bright light. Pet owners should also invest in a lamp. The pet's cage will double as a hospital cage if they are the only resident. The lamp should be mounted on its stand about 15-20cm (6-8in) from the cage bars, and at one end of the cage. This allow the patient to move away from the direct heat if it becomes uncomfortable.

It is best if the lamp can be wired through a thermostat to regulate the temperature. If not, keep the lamp on until the bird is well, otherwise on/off situations will prove counterproductive (temperature fluctuations). The required temperature is 85-90 degrees F (29-32 degrees C). This alone can work wonders, for example for chills, and egg-bound hens. Once the bird is well, it is important to reduce the temperature slowly over a few days, especially if the patient is to be returned to an aviary situation.

THE SICKLY BIRD

In spite of your husbandry standards, total protection from potential illness is impossible. Pathogens can be carried to the cage by flies and other insects, via the bird's food and water, via wild bird droppings, vermin, other pets, via yourself on your hands or clothing, and simply by airborne means. Pathogens are always present in the air. Two things defend your birds from being continually ill. One is their immune system; the other is standards of husbandry that keep all these various disease vectors at low levels of incidence.

By continually observing your birds when they eat, drink, move and rest, you will, in most instances, quickly spot the sickly bird before the pathogens can reach highly dangerous levels. Birds show ill health in two ways, physical and behavioural.

PHYSICAL INDICATORS

Sunken, swollen, cloudy, weeping

and closed eyes when not asleep (many causes), swollen or mucous discharging nostrils (many causes), flaky facial appearance (scaly face – a mite infection), raised leg scales (scaly leg– a mite infection), swollen throat (possibly impacted crop), skin or feather swellings (cysts, abscesses), baldness and feather loss (parasites, fungus, nutritional deficiency, old age, but in some cockatiels, especially in American lutinos, could be genetic), deformed beak (scaly face, old age, misalignment – which can be genetic or environmental).

Deformed feet or nails (nutritional, genetic or environmental – incorrect perch size), very liquid faecal matter and stained vent (many causes), swollen abdomen (cancer of internal organs, hernia, intestinal swelling, prolapsed cloaca), vomiting (many causes), difficulty in breathing (many causes – often of a parasitic or fungal origin), sneezing and coughing (many causes), protrusion from vent (prolapsed cloaca, egg-binding, and other problems), loss of weight (many causes), obesity (usually nutritional), paralysis and fits (many causes including heatstroke, nutritional deficiency, poisoning, genetic, and old age).

Watch for any changes in behaviour which may indicate ill health.

BEHAVIOURAL SIGNS

Sometimes these are the only suggestion of a problem – after which the next thing you observe is that the bird is dead. In such instances, if you have many cockatiels, a post-mortem is

The cockatiel will keep its feathers clean by preening

recommended. It may save others from dying.

Signs include general lethargy, loss of or excess appetite, loss of interest in or excess drinking, reluctance about being handled – more noticeable in a pet, vocalisations cease (talking, mimicking), excess scratching, self-mutilation, cannibalism on offspring, unusual aggression towards people or other birds, excessive sleeping or drowsiness, straining to defecate (but could be egg-binding in a hen), incorrect sleeping posture (discussed shortly), disinterest in what is happening around it, lying and sleeping on the cage floor, tail bobbing (pumping) with each breath, (egg-binding, pneumonia, fungal infection) and any other actions such as cage bar biting, or weaving on the perch, which are abnormal.

Note: The normal sleeping/resting position for a bird is on one foot with head turned to the nape of the neck and nestled among ruffled feathers. Sleeping on two feet with head hunched forward is not normal.

WHAT TO DO

Once you think your cockatiel is ill, you must take swift action otherwise it could deteriorate at a rapid pace. If the signs are only minor, it may only be a minor problem that should rectify itself within 12-24 hours. This becomes a judgement call based on experience. If in doubt, and certainly if two or more signs are present, contact your vet rather than gamble with your bird's life. This is especially important with an egg-bound hen who could rapidly die if the egg is not removed. A vet can attend to this.

Note the time and day as well as the signs of the problem. Review all recent happenings that may be part or all of the cause – other ill pets in the house, change of diet, possible bad food, lack of cleaning!, or a new addition to the collection (especially in aviaries where there is no quarantine facility, which there should be).

It is prudent to move your

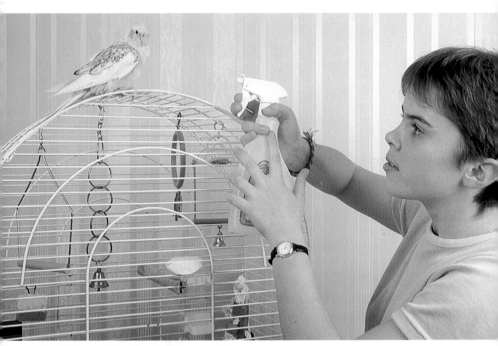

Feathers need to be damp for preening, so a spray with luke-warm water will aid this process.

Ask an expert for help if nails need trimming.

cockatiel away from other birds and pets once they show signs of illness. Gather faecal samples for the vet. Place the cage in a warm location and apply heat treatment. Do not withhold food or water until you have spoken with the vet, though this should be done with soft foods (fruit and those with high moisture content) if the signs are acute diarrhoea. If, after commencing heat treatment, you must visit the vet, wrap the cage in a warm blanket to minimise heat loss.

NAILS AND BEAK

The nails and beak of your cockatiel should be checked to see they do not become overgrown. If diet and perches are correct this should not happen. However, should the nails be overgrown, the tips should be trimmed using manicure or similar clippers. Be careful not to trim too much or the quick will bleed profusely, and cause pain to the bird. A styptic pencil will normally stop this.

With beaks, problems can arise due to genetic misalignment making them over or undershot. If not carefully reshaped, they can grow to an excessive length that can make eating all but impossible. Misalignment may also be caused by bored birds biting on the cage bars. In either case, simply trimming the tip of the beak may be insufficient and profuse bleeding could result if the corium (living core) is cut. A vet should be consulted to reshape the beak.

WOUNDS AND BREAKS
Minor wounds should be bathed and treated with a styptic pencil. Once dry, the wound can be protected from secondary infection with an antiseptic from your vet. Deep wounds will need the vet's immediate treatment. Cover the cut with a surgical gauze to stem the flow. Wrap the bird in towelling to prevent it fluttering and increasing the blood flow.

Minor fractures will normally heal themselves, but major breaks and fractures will need your vet's attention, otherwise the breaks may set at incorrect angles and also lead to arthritis.

PARASITES AND WORMS
Modern drugs, such as Ivermectin, are very effective against a wide range of external parasites and internal worms. They can be given orally or by injection, though the latter can cause birds to go into shock.

A cautionary comment should be made with respect to the misuse of antibiotics. In many popular pets, especially in the USA where certain drugs are more readily available other than via vets, owners often use antibiotics as a preventative. This has resulted in strains of bacteria developing immunity and rendering the drug ineffective when it is most needed. Only use medicines under veterinary supervision.

5 *Training*

Being both intelligent and benign, cockatiels are very easy to finger-train. All further training, other than mimicking sounds, is developed from this. Hopefully, you will have purchased a young bird that is already hand-tame. But it will be assumed this was not the case, so this chapter will tell you exactly how to proceed.

GENERAL COMMENTS

Both cocks and hens are equally easy to train. Cocks, generally, do not nip as hard as hens. Both sexes can mimic sounds, though cocks are usually better and easier to train.

The time it takes to finger-train a cockatiel is variable, because what must be taken into account is the background of the bird, its age, the patience of the owner, and the amount of time devoted to training. These birds can be finger-trained within an hour, or it could take a few days.

WING-CLIPPING

For pet owners there are advantages in clipping the wings of your cockatiel. They are easier to finger-train in this state because, once out of their cage, they cannot fly high enough up to perch out of your reach. However, if dogs, cats or ferrets are also part of your menagerie, wing-clipping is not recommended. It removes the bird's best means of escape – flight.

With clipped wings, the risk of a bird flying at speed into windows, ceiling fans and their like is greatly reduced. The extent of lift is determined by how much of the feather, and how many feathers, are clipped. It is not cruel to clip the wings because the cut feathers will be replaced at the next moult (a point to remember), so you are always able to give the bird full flight once it is well trained.

The practice of clipping only the feathers of one wing is cruel. The bird is never able to land in the direction it heads for because its flight becomes an arc. Eventually, the pet loses all desire even to attempt flight, which is very sad, and very unnatural.

When clipping, you should leave the first one or two outermost primaries intact. Never trim too much from the other feathers, because you may cause them to bleed near the quill base. For neatness, trim alternate feathers and there will be no outward sign that the feathers are clipped.

Remember, the object is not to make the bird flightless, merely to restrict its ability to gain too much lift until it has become very familiar with life in a home. Have your vet or an experienced parrot owner show you how to attend to this if you are apprehensive.

MAKING A START
The best time to commence training is in the evening when the bird is becoming a little tired. It should be done in a quiet room where there are no distractions from people, radios, other pets, TV and the like. This will allow the bird's total attention to focus on you.

Prior to this you should have ensured the bird is settled in its new home. It should not panic when you are near its cage. If it does, your first need is to let it become familiar with your being in close proximity. When this does not bother it, offer tidbits through the cage bars. Confidence-building is then in progress.

MAKING CONTACT
When you are satisfied that the bird is familiar with your presence, the next step is to slowly place your hand, holding a tidbit, into the cage. Let it rest near a perch. Do not move it; let the bird come to take the treat. Sometimes, considerable patience is needed. Only when the bird has no problems perching near your hand to take tidbits should you move to the next stage.

While it is eating its delicacy, move your index finger to just below its chest, above its legs; it will no doubt view this with caution and may move away. If so, leave your hand in the cage and offer another tidbit. It will eventually come for this. Now, through repetition, there will come a time when it will allow you to press your finger against its chest, when you should gently push upwards.

The bird has no alternative but

Step One: Allow your cockatiel to get used to your hand.

Step Two: In time, the cockatiel will hop on to your out-stretched hand.

The cocktail is now quite confident, and will perch quietly while he is being taken out of the cage.

to either flutter away or to step on to your finger. It will usually do the latter. You have now made the breakthrough and will feel a tremendous sense of achievement.

REMOVAL FROM CAGE

Only when the cockatiel is very happy to step onto your finger while in its cage should you attempt to take it out of its home.

Do this very slowly. The first time or two it may flutter back into the cage as you are about to take it out on your finger. But, again, patience achieves all and it will eventually be happy to stay on your finger. Once out, it will usually take a look around, then take flight, or clamber up the cage.

HOUSEHOLD DANGERS

The moment a bird is free to fly in one or more rooms, there are many dangers you must be aware of. Make these safe before the bird is allowed out. The following include most of the likely hazards.

Open windows and fireplaces, glass which the bird may crash into, such as mirrors or windows. Close the curtains or cover the glass with mesh the first time the bird is free. Poisonous house plants that may be nibbled, aquariums with no hoods, open toilets or baths and sinks full of water, cooler or extractor fans, kitchen hobs, boiling pans, open tins of paint or other dangerous liquids, hot irons, cats and dogs are all possible hazards.

It is wise to remove cherished fragile ornaments on shelves which the bird may flutter into. It should also be mentioned that the non-stick surfaces of many cooking pots, as well as paint, irons and heat lamps, often feature Polytetrafluoroethylene (PTFE). The toxic fumes from this are potentially lethal to birds even when the appliance is operated at recommended temperatures. The kitchen is not a good location for a birdcage, nor a good place for birds to be in.

RETURNING TO CAGE

When it is time for the pet to be returned to its cage, approach it slowly and with a tidbit. It will not step down on to your finger so be sure it is able to step upwards. Return it to the cage door and it will usually flutter in. However, it may not wish to end its time out and will flutter away! In such instances, it will test your patience. As a last resort, dim the room and then, when it is on your finger, it will usually stay there until back in its cage. Alternatively, you must close both your hands around its body and firmly but gently transport it back to its little home.

ADVANCED PETTING

Once your cockatiel has no problems stepping on to your finger it is a good idea simply to sit with it while you read or watch

The inquisitive cockatiel will take an interest in everything that is going on.

TV. It will climb on your shoulder, head and body. You will slowly be able to touch its wings, rub its chest, and its neck, which parrots love. Remember, birds do not initially like their wings being touched, so it is a sure sign of progress when you can do this. Eventually, you should be able to place it on its back while you gently play with it, but this takes a lot of trust on the bird's part so do not try to rush any part of training.

PET OWNER'S GUIDE TO THE COCKATIEL

THE GREAT OUTDOORS

Never take your cockatiel outdoors unless it is in its cage. It will take flight and that will usually be the last time you will see it. Even with clipped wings it may still be able to get sufficient lift to clear a fence and flutter into danger. It will, however, enjoy being outdoors in its cage on warm days. Ensure part of the cage is shaded so it can retreat from the sun when it wishes.

MIMICKING SOUNDS

While cockatiels are not the best of the mimics in the parrot family, they can be taught to learn many words. They also become accomplished at mimicking the whistling songs of other birds. Teaching them to talk requires the same solitude as when finger-training. Repeat one or two single words when you have their attention. Do not attempt to teach sentences until they have mastered single words. It requires a great deal of repetition.

Likewise, repetition is the key to teaching them to whistle a tune. As far back as the 1920s, the famed bird authority C.P. Arthur observed that if, after listening to a whistled tune, a young cockatiel shakes its head, it will learn the tune in half the time of a bird that does not do this. Another hint is that the letter H is difficult for these birds to mimic.

Finally, always remember to say the words the way you want the cocky to say them. By this I mean that if you want the pet to say "I am very pretty" you must say that, not "you are very pretty" or that is what it will say. Be aware, also, these birds may learn sounds you do not want them to repeat, which includes screaming babies, barking dogs, and profanities. Be careful what you say on a regular basis when your pet is around!

6 *Breeding Cockatiels*

Although cockatiels are among the easiest of birds to breed, you should not rush into this side of the hobby until you have given due thought to its full implications. This is a fault with many a beginner. All too often they start on a wave of enthusiasm which quickly wanes as one problem adds to another. On the other hand, if you start by appreciating realities, you will no doubt stay in the hobby and become one of its many devoted enthusiasts.

REALITIES

If you are thinking you can make some extra cash breeding cockatiels, you should think again. There is a surfeit of breeders, which suppresses prices. You would be lucky indeed if you even approached break-even on your investment. Breeding must be something you enjoy and are prepared to finance to a greater or lesser degree. At anything more than very low-key levels, breeding consumes a great deal of time. It requires dedication, patience, and an ability to cope with problems.

Most of all, the desire to be steadily improving the quality of your stock must remain. Yet this should never result in the general quality of life of the birds becoming a secondary consideration. This can easily happen. It results in birds having to live out most of their lives in the confines of small breeding cages because the owner has far more pairs than they have outdoor, or even indoor, flights for.

START CORRECTLY

The most common errors with novices is that they start prematurely, with inadequate facilities, an impatience to get breeding underway, and mediocre stock. The recipe for failure is

there from the outset. It is essential that the aviary, birdroom, equipment and appliances conducive to efficiency are purchased ahead of the birds. If cash is limited, make progress in stages, so, when the birds are obtained, everything is in place.

This is especially important if you wish to develop a small stud of exhibition birds, or to specialise in colour mutations. In both instances you will need spare stock cages, individual flights for each pair, ample seed bins, storage cupboards, feeders, a hospital cage, and a quarantine area away from your main birdroom.

While you are developing this facility, you should devote time to studying more in-depth books on breeding, as well as researching who will be a good supplier for your foundation stock.

INITIAL STOCK

Like begets like. Mediocre birds will produce their own kind. Never commence with such birds. Even quality cockatiels will produce some inferior offspring, but they will also have the potential to produce birds of their own, or better, quality. Nor should you assume that a show-winning bird will necessarily be worth

owning as a breeding prospect.

It is a classic error. Clearly, a winning bird has inherited the genes that give it its superior appearance. This does not mean it will pass those genes to its offspring. It could be the only decent bird from an aviary full of very ordinary stock. What you need are birds that come from a stud in which the overall quality is very consistent. Here there is a high probability that any pairs will pass on their genes to all their progeny.

The breeder should have records that you can inspect. These will have little meaning to you, though they indicate that the breeder does monitor their programme. Prospective pairs should be obtained from the same breeder.

They will likely be linebred, which is inbred at a more dilute level. If you obtain good-looking linebred birds from separate studs, you could undo all that each breeder has achieved if you pair them. You will probably still retain some common areas of quality in the resulting stock on which you can build. But it is best to keep lines separate until you learn more about breeding and the genetic principles of inheritance.

Seek expert advice when viewing breeding stock.

VISIT THE BREEDER

You should always visit the breeder so you can see their stud at first hand. In cockatiels there will usually be a good one within your locality. They will be a mine of help when problems arise, and will be near enough for you to purchase extra birds from them at a later date.

Only purchase initial stock sight unseen from a breeder whose reputation you have established is beyond reproach. Attend shows, purchase the catalogue, and you can locate a local breeder, or one with a good reputation who may be too far to visit.

A final comment on visiting a breeder is this. If they had no aviaries, and only modest indoor flights, I would not buy from them. Having access to outdoor flights results in hardy birds. Those bred from one generation to the next in a cocooned, temperature-controlled, birdroom environment, can lose the ability to withstand anything but cocooned environments. They may not survive when placed in year-round outdoor aviaries, especially if this is done in the early autumn.

PROVEN OR NOT?

As a general rule it is best to start with unproven youngsters – birds with no previous breeding record. This is because it gives you time to become familiar with the whole business of running a small aviary or breeding set-up. Also, the birds will be familiar with their home, diet and all else in their environment by the time they reach breeding age.

However, if you have experience with other birds, have begun as recommended in this chapter, and have located a very trustworthy breeder, then obtaining proven birds is a sound strategy. It has the advantage that your initial birds will be more assessable, meaning their appearance will be established, and not hoped for as with youngsters.

If they carry a closed metal leg ring you will be able to establish with certainty their age, otherwise you must take the word of the breeder. An alternative is to purchase proven adults, as well as unproven individuals from the same source. This is also sound strategy, because you can pair the proven adults with the youngsters once they reach breeding age.

Buying proven birds from other than a reputable breeder is a much more risky venture. The birds could be old, they may be feather-pluckers, or have a background of deserting their chicks. They may be finicky eaters. There are no short cuts to purchasing quality birds. As with pet cockatiels, be prepared to pay the going rate for good birds, from a reputable breeder. You will rarely have reason to regret such an investment.

BREEDING AGE

Cockatiels must be fully mature before they are bred. This will be when they are over one year old. Attempts at earlier breeding are unwise. It is poor husbandry to expect birds not yet physically mature to cope with the tremendous strain on their metabolism and physique. It dramatically increases the potential for sickly chicks, and many other problems. If a cockatiel is under strain before it is mature, the resulting deficiencies can never be corrected later on.

BREEDING CONDITION

It is essential that only extremely fit birds are used for breeding. They must never be overweight, nor displaying poor feathers, which is a sure sign of problems.

Obese hens are more likely to become egg-bound (see Health chapter), or lay soft-shelled eggs. A cockatiel cannot attain full fitness in the confines of a small cage. It must have access to at least an indoor flight, and preferably a lengthy outdoor one. However, once fit, they can be bred in a cage with no problems.

NESTBOX

The breeding season (outdoors) commences in the early spring and lasts throughout the summer. Once the birds are ready to be bred they should be given a suitable nestbox which will trigger the breeding process. Its dimensions are flexible. As a guide it should be 31-38cm (12-15in) tall and 23cm (9in) square. An entrance hole about 7.5cm (3in) diameter should be placed a few inches below the top, and slightly to one side of centre. A landing perch is, of course, needed at the hole. If the nestbox is sited in an aviary flight, a sloping roof will more rapidly remove rain. Ensure the roof has an overhang and the nestbox is made of stout timber.

It is best if the nestbox can be taken apart after the breeding season to be thoroughly cleaned. It is also useful, in the taller

A suitable nestbox must be provided.

nestboxes, to nail narrow wooden slats on the inner side of the entrance wall. This allows the youngsters to clamber out of the box more easily when they are ready. Do not use weld mesh; the birds could get their claws trapped in this with tragic results.

The base of the nestbox should feature a wooden concave like those sold for budgerigars. This keeps the eggs safer from scattering and the resultant possible lack of incubation. It also prolongs the life of the nestbox base. A hinged inspection door just above the height of the concave, and opposite the entrance hole, is a useful feature. It enables you quickly to inspect the nest when the parents are both out of it.

In a cage location, an external nest box is preferred: it makes nest inspection easier and leaves more room in the cage for the birds. The concave obviates the need for nesting material, but a few shavings or peat can be added to help absorb liquid faecal matter. Do not use cedar or pine shavings. They are potentially very harmful. The phenols they contain can be released, once damp. These will adversely affect the respiratory and other systems of birds and small mammals.

In an aviary, site the nestbox in a protected, yet relatively open, site; cockatiels do not like dark, heavily foliaged areas. Place two nestboxes in different sites so the birds have a choice. Sometimes the direction a nestbox faces can be important to particular pairs.

CAGE SIZE

If breeding in a cage, it should have good size – about 1.3m (4ft) length with height and depth as discussed in the housing chapter.

CLUTCH SIZE

A typical clutch will comprise four to six white eggs, though it is possible for as many as eight or more to be laid. Large clutches will rarely all be reared, so it is best to transfer any above five or six to a foster bird, if one is available with a small clutch. The eggs are laid on alternate days.

INCUBATION

Incubation normally begins after the first or second egg is laid. Both sexes share this job. The female sits during the night while the male sleeps on the perch at the entrance. He will sit during the day. Sometimes both will sit together during the day. The incubation time is variable, 18 to 21 days being typical.

REARING CHICKS

Both parents share the rearing duties. After about ten days the parents cease brooding for part of the day. Sometimes, with first-time parents, one or both of them may fail to incubate and brood as they should. If the first clutch of eggs proves a failure, do not be overly worried. The second or third clutch will normally be reared without problems.

Cockatiels fledge when about four to five weeks of age and should be eating independently of

1. Incubation lasts between 18-21 days.

3. The chicks have started to hatch.

2. Seven days old.

4. A white faced pied chick at 26 days.

their parents shortly after this. Only when you are sure they are eating independently should they be separated from the parents, who by then will probably have a second clutch of eggs in the nestbox.

LEG RINGS

There are two types of rings or bands which can be placed on the legs of chicks for identification purposes. Closed metal rings are fitted when the chicks are 8 to 12 days of age. They serve as a permanent record of the bird's age, and can be numbered to identify individual birds. They can be obtained from your national cockatiel society, or from specialist sellers. They must be the correct size for cockatiels.

A breeder will show you how to fit these rings over the legs of the chicks. The second type of ring, available in metal or plastic, is the split ring. These can be single or double-coloured and they serve numerous purposes, such as identifying given cocks and hens, or birds to be retained, or sold, and so on.

When birds are closed rung it is essential you always check that the rings are never clogged with debris or faecal matter. This can cause the leg to swell. Unless remedied promptly the bird could lose its leg. If the leg swells, let your vet cut the ring and treat the bird. Split rings are easily placed on the legs, or removed, at any time. Some breeders will not use closed rings, but they are required on exhibition birds in most countries and, actually, rarely create problems.

BREEDING RECORDS

No worthwhile breeding programme can be undertaken without accurate breeding records being maintained. You can purchase standard registers from national societies or design your own. They will create a complete history of your birds, and help in developing breeding strategies.

SELECTION

The golden key to being a successful breeder is having the ability to select worthwhile birds for retention and for future breeding. Unless this skill can be developed, any quality you have in the initial stock will vanish in future breedings.

There are many methods you can use to assess birds or their offspring. All rely heavily on your ability to assess your stock critically and not get carried away by minor attributes. Seek out genetic books which include chapters on methods of selection. The books do not need to be specific to cockatiels: selection methods apply to all forms of livestock.

EXHIBITING

For many breeders, showing their birds is an essential part of the hobby. It is a way of assessing the success of a breeding programme in a competitive manner. However, only a very small percentage of cockatiel owners and breeders involve themselves in this side of the hobby. Nonetheless, it is a vital part of the avicultural scene.

In order to be successful, a bird must be super-fit and be an excellent example of its variety, based on the official standard of the society under whose rules it is exhibited. It must be well trained in order to spend many hours in a show cage and show itself to best advantage to the judge. To achieve such a status involves a great deal of extra work by the breeder, as well as time and cost travelling to the shows.

Many breeders who like showing, but do not have the time to do it, will form partnerships with a person who handles the exhibition side. Many such unions prove highly successful. All breeders, and pet owners, even if they have no desire to exhibit, are recommended to visit shows. It is a great day out and you will meet lots of other cockatiel enthusiasts, and keep abreast of what is happening in the world of the cockatiel.

One Stop Reference

Common Name: Cockatiel.

Synonyms: Quarrion, Weero, Cockatoo Parrot, Crested Parrot, Corella, Grey & Yellow Top-knotted Parrot, Crested Red-cheeked Nymphious, Ground Parakeet, Cockateel.

Distribution: Throughout Australia with exception of some coastal areas.

Scientific Name: *Nymphicus hollandicus.*

Order: Psittaciformes.

Family: Cacatuidae.

No. Species: One.

Total Length: 30-36 cm (11.8-14in). (Not including crest of about 6.3cm [2 2/5in]).

Tail Length: 14-17 cm (5 1/2-6.7in).

Wing Size: 16-18 cm (6 1/2-7in).

Claws: Zygodactyl (two face forwards, two backwards).

Weight: Birth 4.5g Weaning 70g (21/2oz) Adult 80-110g (2.8-3.9oz).

Sexual Distinction: The sexes are dimorphic, meaning differing in appearance.

Longevity: 15-20 years typical, but may attain 25, or even more years.

Nestbox Type: Hollow log or nestbox with pan: Typical dimensions 31-38x23x23cm (12-15x9x9in).

Recommended Breeding Age: 12 months or older.

Average Clutch: 4-6 (range 1-10) laid on alternate days. Eggs white.

Incubation: 18-21 days. Both sexes share incubation duties.

Eyes Open: About 8 days.

Ringing (Banding) Age: 6-10 days (Int. ring diameter 5mm).

Fledging Age: 28-35 days (4-5 weeks).

Adult Plumage: Approx. 6 months.

Sexual Maturity: 6-7 months.

Clutches Per Year: 4 (2 rounds) is recommended maximum.

Compatibility: Very social within own species, and with others. Safe with smaller birds. May be bullied by those larger than themselves.

Diet: Mixed seed, greens, fruits.

Perch Size: 9.5-19mm (3/8-3/4in).

Heart Rate: 360-420 beats per minute.

Respiration Rate: 100-120 beats per minute.

Body Temp (Day): 42°C (107.6°F).

Pet Rating: Outstanding. Male generally makes the better pet.

Wild Colour Pattern: This is termed 'normal' or 'wild type' within the avicultural hobby. It is grey with yellow crest, orange cheek spots, and some white and yellow in the wing and tail-feathers.

Mutational Colours: There are a number of mutational colours/patterns. These include single mutations and combinations (composites) of these, of which there are many. The most well-known mutational forms are:

Lutino (yellow) (genetically partial albino)

Cinnamon

Silver

Pied

Whitefaced

Albino (genetically a white)

Pearled

Fallow

Yellow-faced

Pastel-faced

Pearl-Pied

Purchase Price: The cockatiel, with the exception of the budgerigar, is the least expensive of all 330 species of parrot-like birds (based on normal [wild type] colour pattern).

Recommended Purchase Age: Whether for a pet or breeding, the best age to obtain a cockatiel is after it has fledged and is eating independently of parents. 6-10 weeks is ideal.

Cockatiel: One-Stop Reference
Copyright: Dennis Kelsey-Wood